SHOW ME THE WAY TO SPAIN

GEOGRAPHY BOOK 1ST GRADE
CHILDREN'S EXPLORE THE WORLD BOOKS

BABY PROFESSOR
EDUCATION KIDS

Speedy Publishing LLC

40 E. Main St. #1156

Newark, DE 19711

www.speedypublishing.com

Copyright 2017

In this book, we're going to talk about places to visit in Spain. So, let's get right to it!

In the country of Spain there are so many interesting things to do. You can eat delicious tapas, which are tiny, bite-sized foods. You can watch flamenco dancers as they stomp their feet and dance to the music. You can listen to music in the street during a festival called a fiesta. You can wander the streets and look at ancient buildings that have stood for centuries. Spain is a country that is filled with culture as well as history and tradition.

Spanish Square (Plaza de Espana) in Sevilla, Spain

View of the center of Barcelona, Spain

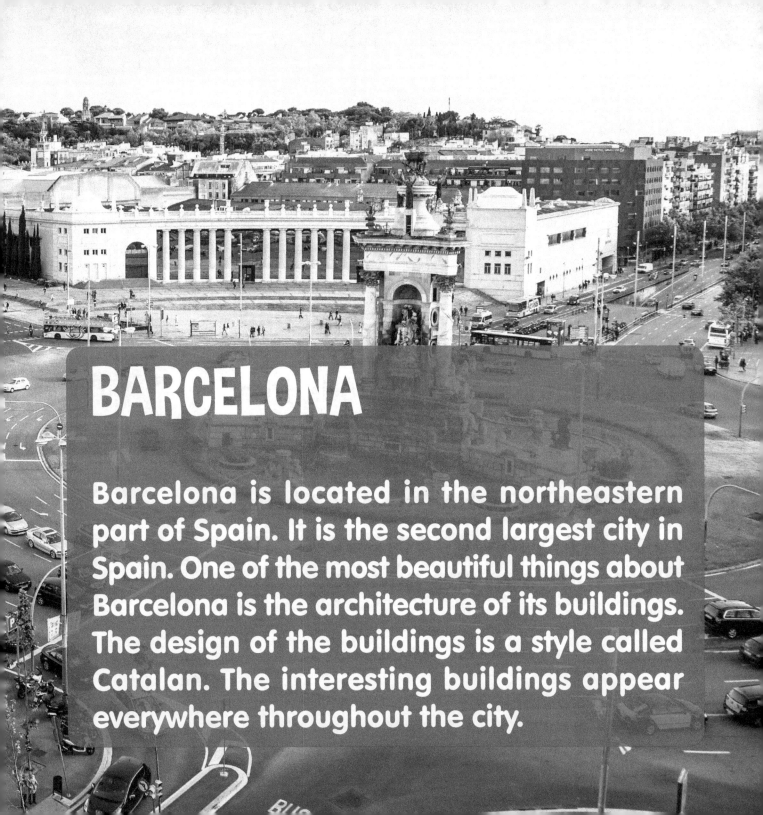

BARCELONA

Barcelona is located in the northeastern part of Spain. It is the second largest city in Spain. One of the most beautiful things about Barcelona is the architecture of its buildings. The design of the buildings is a style called Catalan. The interesting buildings appear everywhere throughout the city.

You can hop on the metro and travel all around Barcelona to see interesting neighborhoods like Les Corts or Sant Andreu. If you're adventurous, you might want to walk to the neighborhood of Ciutat Vella. Every neighborhood has unique things to see and do.

The Parc de la Ciutadella. It is a park on the northeastern edge of Ciutat Vella

Escalivada

If you like to try new foods, you should try the Catalan cuisine of this area. Two popular foods are:

- Escalivada, which are smoky grilled vegetables
- Escudella i carn d'olla, which is a traditional soupy stew with a giant meatball that has been part of the cuisine since the 14th century

Famous city of Bilbao, Spain

BILBAO

Bilbao is a seaport city in Northern Spain. Just as Barcelona represents the Catalan culture, Bilboa is the gateway to the Basque culture.

One of the most fascinating places to visit is the Museo Guggenheim Bilbao. The amazing design of this building looks like giant pieces of metal ribbon that are curved. It was Architect Frank Gehry's design and it became famous.

Flower puppy

The Museum has an enormous collection of modern art with lots of interesting pieces including:

- **Humans by Christian Boltanski,** which is an indoor display with hundreds of black and white photographs of people
- **Maman by Louise Bourgeois,** which is an outdoor sculpture that looks like a gigantic spider
- **Puppy by Jeff Koons,** which is an outdoor metal frame with soil and flowering plants that looks like a gigantic puppy

BURGOS

Burgos is a quiet and serene city in the northern part of Spain. The city has a rich heritage that goes back to 884 AD when it was founded. It is nicknamed the "Land of Castles" because of its monuments from medieval times. Two of those monuments are:

- The Cartuja de Miraflores, which is a beautiful monastery with tall spires built in 1401 AD

Cartuja de Miraflores Monastery

Gothic Cathedral

- **The Abbey of Santa Maria la Real de Las Huelgas, which was founded in 1187 AD and is one of the original dwellings where nuns lived in Spain**

Another popular place to visit is the Catedral de Burgos, which as been called the most beautiful example of a Gothic cathedral in Spain. It was originally built in 1230 AD.

CORDOBA

Cordoba is an inland seaport that is located on the Guadalquivir River. It was established by the Romans and some of their designs, such as Roman arches, can still be seen in the city. Eventually, the city was taken over by the Muslims and they built beautiful buildings when they made the city the capital of their kingdom called Al-Andalus. It's considered to be one of the most beautiful of Spain's cities.

River Guadalquivir in Cordoba

The Mezquita of Cordoba

It was so magnificent that when the Christians took it back from the Muslims in the year 1236 AD, they left most of the city's amazing architecture standing.

One of the most interesting buildings is the Mezquita, which was built as an Islamic mosque. It was used for different religions at a time when Muslims, Jews, and Christians all worshipped side by side.

GIRONA

Girona is located in the northern part of Spain close to the Pyrenees Mountains and by the River Onyar. Part of the city is surrounded by a majestic wall. It has lovely, large squares and cobblestone streets for sightseeing. It also has lots of historical buildings. The beaches of Costa Brava are about a 20-minute drive by car.

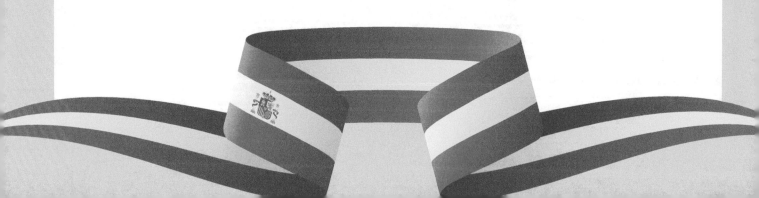

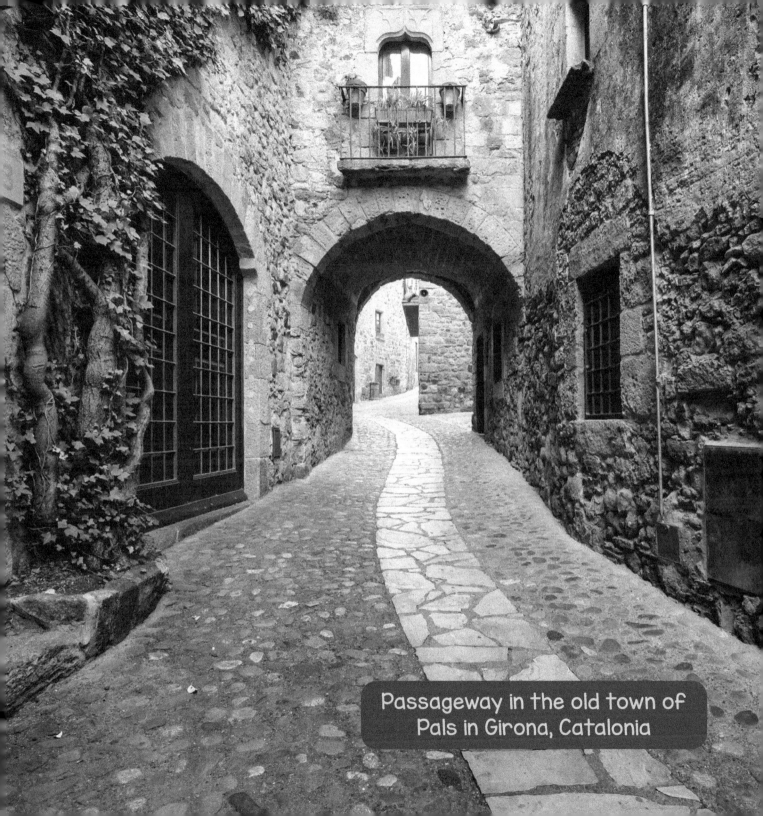

Passageway in the old town of Pals in Girona, Catalonia

Many people think the beaches in Spain are the most beautiful in the world. Some of the most interesting places to see in Girona are:

- Força Vella, which are the remains of a fortress built by the Romans
- The Arab Baths, built in 1194 AD
- Sant Pere de Galligants, which has a beautiful bell tower and strange animals as well as creatures from mythology on the tops of its columns

Monastery of Sant Pere de Galligants

- **Sant Nicolau, a chapel built in the 12th century**
- **Passeig Arqueologic, which has lovely walkways with gardens**

Castell de Sant Nicolau

Historical city of Granada, Spain

GRANADA

The city of Granada is located near the Sierra Nevada Mountains. It's in the southern region of Spain that is called Andalusia. It has been called the "Land of a Thousand Castles" because of the beautiful buildings constructed there by the Arabs. They claimed it in the 8th century, but the Christians took the city back in 1492.

One of the major sights is the Alhambra, which is a spectacular palace and fortress complex. It's believed that a spirit lives within its ancient walls.

Alhambra Palace, Granada, Spain

Ordesa y Monte Perdido National Park

HUESCA

The city of Huesca is situated in the northeastern region of Spain called Aragon.

People who love adventure and skiing come to this beautiful mountainous region for two famous resorts, Formigal and Candanchú. The resorts are crowded with skiers from all over the world in the winter months. Hikers come to see the beautiful scenery in Ordesa y Monte Perdido National Park, which has towering summits.

JEREZ DE LA FRONTERA

Jerez is located in southwestern Spain. If you want to see traditional flamenco dancing, this is the place to visit. The lively flamenco music and the dancers with their quick, rhythmic steps fill the streets. Jerez is also an important city for Andalusian horses. This amazing type of horse is a pure Spanish breed whose ancestors lived on the Iberian Peninsula for thousands of years.

Beautiful carriage horses
in Jerez, Spain

Facade of the Cathedral of Santiago de Compostela

LOGRONO

Logroño is one of the most ancient cities in Spain and some of its buildings date back to the Middle Ages. Much of its history is tied to the route that faithful Christian pilgrims would take to Santiago de Compostela to visit the grave of the Apostle known as James the Great. Logroño was an important resting spot along the way.

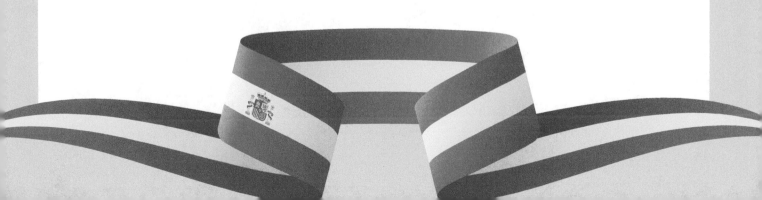

There are many historic squares that have special buildings such as:

- The Cathedral of Santa Maria la Redonda, which has two towers and historic art
- The Church of Santiago, which is dedicated to Saint James and is the oldest church in the city
- The Pilgrim's Shelter, where pilgrims stayed to rest from their travels

After a long day of sightseeing in Logroño, you can have delicious marzipan or pastries made with almonds for a snack.

Cathedral of Saint Maria de la Redonda in Logrono

El Prado Museum

MADRID

The city of Madrid is located right in the center of Spain and is its capital city. It's a huge city and over 4 million people live there. The biggest draw for visitors coming to Madrid are its many amazing art museums. The three top museums are:

- The Prado, which has one of the world's finest European art collections dating from as early as the 12th century

- **The Reina Sofia, which houses 20th century art**
- **The Thyssne-Bornemisza, which was started as a private collection**

These three museums form a "golden triangle" of art since they are located so close together.

Madrid is also known for its many cafés and flea markets. At night, there are lively parties and disco music everywhere.

Cityscape of Ourense City

OURENSE

Ourense is located in northwestern Spain. The city doesn't have many tourists so it's great for a one or two day trip to relax and explore. The old town section is an easy walk over a day's time and there are lots of ancient monasteries and stone forts to discover.

SALAMANCA

Salamanca is located in the western part of Spain within the region that's called Castile y León. The city has a student culture because one of the oldest Spanish universities is there. It's called the Universidad de Salamanca.

Salamanca, Spain

Convent of Santa Teresa

There are beautiful religious buildings in the older section of the city including:

- **The Iglesia de San Juan de Barbalos**
- **The Convent of Las Claras**
- **The Convent of Santa Teresa**

After classes are out, on the other side of town, the restaurants are filled with students relaxing after their studies.

SANTILLANA DEL MAR

Santillana del Mar is located on the west coast of the region of Cantabria, Spain. If you would like to see how a medieval village looked in the era between the 14th through 18th centuries, then you'll have fun exploring this historic city by foot.

Santillana del Mar

Decorated marquee tents at the April fair in Seville, Spain

SEVILLE

The city of Seville is located on the Guadalquivir River and is the largest city in the south of Spain. If you love festivals, Seville is a great place to visit. Every year entertainers perform in the amazing Feria de Abril, which is Spain's most colorful festival.

VALENCIA

Valencia is the third largest city of Spain in terms of population. Madrid is the largest and Barcelona is the second largest. Valencia is home to the traditional dish of paella, which is a delicious dish of chicken, sausage, shrimp and yellow saffron rice.

Spanish Seafood Paella Rice Dish

SPAIN'S RICH HISTORY

The cities of Spain are filled with history and culture from coast to coast. The world's major religious groups including Muslims, Jews, and Christians have all lived there and have shaped the architecture, art, history, and culture of this amazing country. The coastlines have beautiful beaches and skiers enjoy the scenic mountain resorts. The tapas will tempt your taste buds and your ears will love the rhythmic music and dancing of the traditional flamenco.

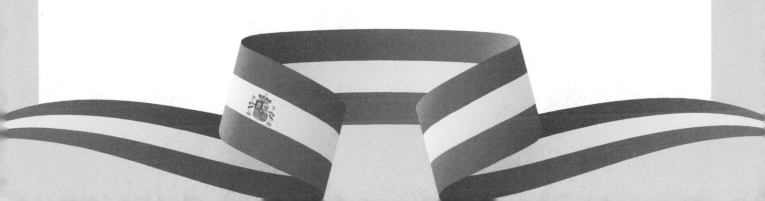

Awesome! Now that you know more about the country of Spain you may want to find out more about the country of France in the Baby Professor book Say Hi to Eiffel! Places to Go in France—Geography for Kids.

SPAIN

9 781541 915831